The UK Air Fryer Cookbook for Beginners and Pros

Easy and Delicious Recipes for Family and Friends incl. Special Air Fryer Desserts

Olivia Burnell

ISBN - 9798480960846

TABLE OF CONTENTS

Introduction

Since they first hit the market in 2010, air fryers have rapidly become one of the most popular kitchen gadgets. They cook food with the crispness and flavour of a deep fat fryer but use only a fraction of the oil, and so are a much healthier cooking option. An air fryer is so much more than a deep fat fryer though, and you can cook a whole range of foods in it. This book shares loads of ideas and recipes to show you how to make the most of your air fryer.

All about Air Fryers

What is an Air Fryer?

The fryer stands on a worktop and plugs into a normal electrical socket and cooks by circulating very hot air over and around the food – a bit like a fan oven but smaller and using a higher concentration of hot air which crisps the food as it cooks. Depending on what you are cooking, you will sometimes need to add a small amount of oil. The food is cooked in an enclosed space so your kitchen will not get hot, although some steam may be released (More on how to avoid this in All about Oils.)

What Can I Cook in My Air Fryer?

You can cook anything that is normally deep fried, but you can also roast potatoes and other vegetables. Air fryers are great for reheating and recrisping foods that have gone soggy, and for cooking various frozen foods, such as potato fries and vegetables. Your air fryer can cook meat, steaks, fillets of fish, as well as biscuits, small cakes and donuts to name but a few favourites! Believe it or not, you can also use your fryer to cook frittatas and other egg-based dishes, as well as for roasting seeds. You will find recipes for all these things and more in the Recipes section of this book. Things to avoid are leafy greens, and liquids such as batter – anything that is battered is best cooked from frozen in your fryer.

Which is the Best Air Fryer for me?

There is a huge range of air fryers to choose from, so it's easy to get overwhelmed. Ask yourself the following questions to narrow the options down:

- How many people will I be cooking for?
- What will I use it for? (I suggest you take a look at some of the ideas in this book before you answer that one!)
- How often will I be cooking with it?
- Can I use a compatible baking tin, bowl or tray? (Important if you want to cook cakes or biscuits)
- Where will I store it? (Think about the size of the fryer – they come in all shapes and sizes)

The rest of this section provides some more information to help you decide.

Price

There are many models on the market ranging in price from around £40 to over £200. The least expensive air fryers have limited capacity and are best if you are cooking for one or cooking foods from frozen.

Basket and Oven Style Air Fryers

There are two types of air fryers: the **basket air fryer** (these come in a variety of shapes and sizes) which has a drawer that slides out to access the basket. Some of these basket air fryers also come with paddles which will turn and rearrange the food for you. The second type are **convection oven air fryers** (these look more like microwave ovens). Convection oven air fryers act as an air fryer and small oven combination; some have the capacity to cook several trays of food at once and can even accommodate a rotisserie device. These air fryer/ oven combos tend to function more like a traditional convection oven and can get very messy. The recipes and advice in this book refer to basket-style, drawer, air fryers, and assume that they don't have paddles.

How Hi-Tech Do You Want to Be?

Some air fryers have manual controls while others have touch screens. Also, many come with preset programmes, so if you prefer to work out your own cooking times this might be a facility that you won't use. If you want to go really hi-tech maybe go for a fryer that has Wi-Fi – this will allow you to download an app that you can programme and set in advance. However, you will still need to be around to shake the basket every so often, so there is not much advantage unless you have an appliance with a paddle that does the rearranging for you.

Size and Capacity

Basket capacity can be anything from 1 to 7 litres, and the larger models have baskets that can accommodate anything up to a small chicken – although cooking a whole chicken in an air fryer is not recommended. Air fryers work best with smaller items that can cook through quickly. The size of your fryer and the amount of food you are cooking will have some effect on the cooking time, but most fryer recipes take 10–30 minutes to cook. If you overload your fryer, the food won't crisp up and will become chewy and unpleasant to eat. To get the most out of an air fryer, it's best to go for a model that has a compatible bowl, tray and baking tin. The recipes in this book assume that you have these items (See Air Fryer Accessories.)

How Do I Use My Air Fryer?

Getting Started

When you unpack your air fryer you will probably find that it comes with a basket (often a bowl with lots of holes in it) and a tray (or a grate) that may sit in the bottom of the basket or underneath it, also with many holes – this is where any excess fat drains away.

Some models will advise that you heat them without any food before cooking anything, to get rid of any smells. Air fryers generally only take about 3 or 4 minutes to heat, and although some recipes advise preheating, it's up to you. When you've got used to your fryer you may find that preheating isn't needed as it reaches the temperature quite quickly.

Place the fryer on a counter top least 7–8cm from the wall. The rear of the appliance can get hot and will need space for the heat to disperse.

General Cooking Advice

Most recipes will include 5–10 ml oil, depending on the ingredients. You will need to coat the food with oil before cooking so the fryer will crisp your food. Some recipes advise spraying the inside of the basket rather than the items themselves. It's often worth lining trays and baking tins with baking parchment to avoid sticking (See Air Fryer Accessories.)

When chopping or slicing vegetables, don't have large chunks or pieces as they won't cook through evenly. Vegetables that have a high starch content such as potatoes, parsnips, squash or sweet potato will need to be soaked in water for around 30 minutes and then patted dry to avoid too much moisture and steam building up inside the fryer. Some vegetables, especially potatoes, can be parboiled and then patted dry to enable them to cook through and avoid too much starch. You will find reminders of these points in the individual recipes that use these ingredients.

Arrange the items to be cooked in the basket (or on a tray if the recipe suggests this option) carefully and don't overfill. There needs to be space for the air to circulate around the food. Most recipes will tell you to shake the basket half way through the cooking time, but it's a good idea to shake the basket every five minutes to redistribute the items to enable maximum crispness, so don't put the fryer on and go for a cup of tea – air fryers need quite a lot of attention when they're cooking. Some models will have built-in paddles that will rearrange the food automatically at regular intervals, but until you really know your fryer, it's still better to check manually. Cooking times tend to range from 10 to 30 minutes.

You can open the drawer to check on the food and shake the basket at any time. When you close it the machine will automatically resume cooking – a bit like a dishwasher. Do make sure that you close the drawer fully, however, otherwise the fryer won't restart. Most fryers make a degree of noise so you'll know if it hasn't restarted.

Some parts of the fryer can get hot when cooking, so be careful about touching it until you are used to the appliance. Your kitchen should still remain cool, however, as the cooking time is relatively short. The other thing you might notice is that steam sometimes escapes from the appliance; this often happens if there is quite a bit of moisture in the food or you have used the wrong kind of oil (See A Note on Oils below.)

You may find that your fryer takes a little longer than the time in the recipe to crisp your food, if so, just cook for a further 4 or 5 minutes, checking regularly. As you get to know your fryer you'll know just how long various things take to cook.

When your food is cooked, open the drawer and take the food out of the basket using a spoon, or tongs for individual items. Never tip the food out because the hot oil that has drained through the grate into the bottom of the basket will pour out on top of the food – and no one wants that! Also, it can spit and be very dangerous. And finally, never cook food in plastic containers in the air fryer. It gets very hot and the plastic may well melt.

All about Oils

Hot air alone is not enough to get the delicious crispy but moist effect you're after. All air fryers need a small amount of oil to make the food crispy, and this is either already in the food or you need to coat the food with it yourself. If you cook with no oil, the food will become dry and brittle.

Some oils will perform better than others in your air fryer. Oils with a high smoke point, such as vegetable oil and avocado oil, can tolerate a high heat before they begin to burn. Olive oil is not a good choice as it doesn't tolerate high temperatures and will produce a lot of steam and leave your food tasting a bit strange.

A lot of air fryer users prefer to use oil sprays as they cover the food in a fine mist that results in a more even coating. Oil sprays are found in all larger supermarkets, or you can get a refillable spray container and use your own oil – this might give you a wider choice. When using a spray container always make sure it's a pump-action type, as the chemicals in propellant sprays make your food taste unpleasant and can damage the lining of your fryer. When a recipe suggests 5ml of oil, a couple of pumps from your oil spray will do the job. The recipes in this book suggest spraying as the most effective and least messy method.

What about Frozen Food?

Air fryers come into their own with frozen food and are especially good for cooking small items such as battered chicken balls, meat balls, spring rolls, battered fish or pastries. Larger items such as meat joints or bigger pieces of chicken are best cooked in a conventional oven. Frozen vegetables are often soggy or watery when cooked from frozen in boiling water or in a conventional oven, but using an air fryer will give you tasty and crispy results. You will simply need to preheat your air fryer and spray a little oil on the inside of your air fryer basket or onto the items themselves, arrange in the basket and away you go! As a general rule, 200 degrees is the best temperature to go for and check the items, shaking the basket every 5 minutes, until you get to know the best cooking times for your favourite foods.

Can I Cook Eggs?

Yes, you can cook eggs in a number of ways including omelettes, frittatas or simply as individual eggs. For 'boiled' (technically they're baked rather than boiled) eggs you need to preheat your air fryer to a low temperature – around 130 degrees – and cook the eggs for around 15 minutes. It's best to experiment with 1 or 2 eggs at a time to find out what works best in your particular fryer, depending on whether you like your eggs runny or solid.

What about Seeds?

Air fryers are great for toasting seeds. You can either make several batches, and store them to add to recipes or to sprinkle over dishes, or you can toast just enough for a single use. Simply preheat your air fryer to 170 degrees. Then line the tray or the bottom of the air fryer basket with parchment and spread the seeds evenly in a single layer and spray with 5ml oil. Roast for about 10 minutes shaking the basket or turning the nuts on the tray halfway through. Allow to cool, and you're done.

How Do I Clean and Store My Air Fryer?

You can wipe down the non-removable parts of your fryer with a paper towel but be sure to wash the basket and grate with hot, soapy water – many air fryers now have dishwasher-safe parts. It is important to clean your fryer and to wash removable components after every use, as otherwise any remnants of your previous dish will burn and create an acrid smell when your fryer heats. If you use your air fryer regularly it's best to keep it on the countertop, and so the size of the appliance might be a consideration when you are deciding which model to buy as they vary in size. Equally, if you are going to store it in a cupboard or on a shelf, check the dimensions before you buy.

Air Fryer Accessories

Depending on the model of air fryer you have, there are often optional additional accessories available that will give you a wider range of cooking options. These include:

- Baking tins and bowls – these usually come in either 13.5cm or 17cm widths (often described as 7" and 9" tins or bowls) and should fit inside the air fryer basket. Check your fryer size before buying. A baking pan and bowl will enable you to cook a wider range of dishes, such as cakes or macaroni cheese

- Trays – you may be able to replace your basket with a tray which is great for spacing items out, or you may have a fryer that has a square-shaped basket with a flat bottom which does just as well

- Baking parchment or foil – some air fryer users place a sheet of parchment or foil to line the tray where the oil collects to minimise cleaning, or to line a baking tin to avoid sticking. Parchment is also great for lining trays and baking tins

Check your appliance manual to see what is compatible with your fryer. Some of the recipes in this book assume that you have a baking pan, a bowl or a tray. This might also be a factor in deciding which appliance to buy.

Are Air Fryers Eco-Friendly?

This has become an increasingly important question when people buy appliances, and with climate change very much on everyone's mind at this time, it should be addressed. So, in a word – yes; air fryers are definitely an eco-friendly option. Here are a few of the reasons why:

- They cook and heat up much faster than a conventional oven, using far less power
- When you open the drawer to check the food, the air fryer switches off and then restarts when you close it. With a conventional oven you lose heat when you open the door to check food and then it takes a while to reach the set temperature again
- Less oil means that there is far less waste than a deep fat fryer produces

How Healthy Are Air Fryers?

Everyone agrees that food cooked in an air fryer has less than half the fat of the same food cooked in a deep fat fryer, and that means far fewer calories. Great news for people with type 2 diabetes or heart conditions – although all health professionals agree that you shouldn't live just on food cooked in your air fryer. The dishes you cook need to be part of a balanced diet that includes fresh fruit and vegetables.

Several studies have found that food cooked in an air fryer has lower levels of a substance called acrylamide. This can be a cancer-causing agent and is naturally created when starchy foods, such as potatoes are cooked at high temperatures for a long time. So, reducing the amount of starch by soaking starchy vegetables before cooking, along with shorter cooking times and less oil, are thought to reduce levels of acrylamide.

The Recipes in this Book

The following recipes will give you the number of portions each will make as well as nutritional information relating to fat, carbohydrate, and protein levels. The nutrition values will obviously vary according to the sizes and types of ingredients used and are only intended as a rough guide. They don't include the serving suggestions. The air fryer temperatures are given in degrees Celsius – although some fryers will have a convert-to-Fahrenheit function if that's what you're more comfortable with.

These recipes are based on basket fryers rather than fryer/oven combinations, and assume the availability of a bowl, a tray and a baking tin. The amounts given are for a fryer of average capacity. Depending on the size of your fryer you may need to adapt the amounts in some of the recipes or cook in batches. The more you use your fryer the more you will get to know which cooking times and sizes of cooking batches are best.

Okay. Let's get cooking!

Savoury Snacks and Sides

POTATO FRIES

(SERVES 4)

NUTRITION PER SERVING: CALORIES 120 | FAT 1G | CARBS 5G | PROTEIN 1G

INGREDIENTS:

- 3 large potatoes (Floury potatoes such as King Edward, Maris Piper or Desirée are best for potato fries)
- 5ml oil or 2 pumps of an oil sprayer

PREPARATION:

1. Preheat your air fryer to 200 degrees
2. Peel the potatoes and cut into batons. (Leave the skins on if you prefer – they will crisp up beautifully)
3. Soak the batons for 10 minutes and then rinse and pat dry
4. Spray the potato fries with the oil and add any flavourings you want to add, such as salt and pepper, garlic or paprika seasoning or maybe dried herbs
5. Arrange the potato fries in the air fryer basket. Try to allow maximum space for the hot air to circulate
6. Cook for 20–30 minutes, shaking the basket halfway through. Check after 20 minutes and continue cooking as necessary shaking the basket every 5 minutes
7. For added tastiness, add some grated Parmesan on your final shake
8. Remove the potato fries with a large spoon or tongs

   Serve as a side with almost anything!

   If you want to make chunky potato fries or wedges, cut into thicker shapes, soak well and arrange extra carefully in the bowl. Don't overfill it or your potato fries will be soggy. It might be better to cook them in 2 batches.

ROSEMARY ROASTED VEGETABLES

(SERVES 4)

NUTRITION PER SERVING: CALORIES 70 | FAT 1G |CARBS 2G | PROTEIN 1G

INGREDIENTS:

- 1 yellow pepper
- 1 red pepper
- 1 courgette
- 1 onion
- 1 broccoli head
- 1 teaspoon of dried rosemary
- Salt and pepper to season
- 10ml oil

PREPARATION:

1. Preheat your air fryer to 180 degrees
2. Slice or cube the vegetables but don't have pieces more than 2 cm thick
3. Wash, pat dry, and separate the broccoli into individual florets
4. Toss the vegetables in the dried rosemary and the oil
5. Season to your taste
6. Arrange the ingredients in the air fryer bowl
7. Cook for 10–15 minutes. Shake the basket half way through. Cook for a further 5 minutes if necessary
   Serve as a side dish with meat or fish.

CRISPY ITALIAN COURGETTE FRIES

(SERVES 4)

NUTRITION PER SERVING: 30 CALORIES | FAT 1.5G | CARBS 5G | PROTEIN 2G

INGREDIENTS:
- 1 courgette
- 220g breadcrumbs
- 1 egg
- 100g grated Parmesan
- 4g Italian seasoning powder
- 5–10ml oil

PREPARATION:
1. Preheat your air fryer to 200 degrees
2. Cut the courgette into thin strips or spirals
3. Mix the dry ingredients together
4. Beat the egg
5. Dip the courgette strips into the egg mixture and then the breadcrumb mixture making sure that each strip is coated
6. Spray the strips with the oil
7. Arrange the strips in the air fryer basket so that there is room for the air to circulate
8. Cook for 10 minutes shaking the basket halfway through
   Serve as a side for almost anything or just eat as a snack.

TANGY ROASTED CAULIFLOWER

(SERVES 4)

NUTRITION PER SERVING: CALORIES 60 | FAT 2G | CARBS 6G | PROTEIN 3G

INGREDIENTS:

- ◆ 2 cauliflowers broken into florets (Only use florets for this recipe. Discard the solid part on the centre of the cauliflower)
- ◆ 30ml oil (Peanut or sesame oil works well with this recipe)
- ◆ 2 grated cloves of garlic
- ◆ 4g paprika powder
- ◆ 5ml oil
- ◆ Salt and pepper to season

PREPARATION:

1. Preheat your air fryer to 200 degrees
2. Mix the oil, garlic, paprika and seasoning
3. Rub the mixture into the florets and spray with the oil
4. Arrange the florets in the air fryer basket (Don't overload the basket)
5. Cook for 15 minutes shaking the basket every 5 minutes
   Serve as a side to meat or fish.

CRISPY BRUSSELS SPROUTS

(SERVES 4)

NUTRITION PER SERVING: CALORIES 140 | FAT 8G | CARBS 5G | PROTEIN 4G

INGREDIENTS:

- 450g trimmed and halved Brussels sprouts
- 2g salt
- 3 finely chopped spring onions
- 28g melted butter
- 5ml white wine vinegar
- 5–10 ml oil

PREPARATION:

1. Preheat your air fryer to 190 degrees
2. Spray the sprouts with the oil and season with salt tossing to ensure the sprouts are evenly coated
3. Arrange in the air fryer basket in a single layer and cook for 15 minutes shaking the basket every 5 minutes (You may have to cook these in batches)
4. Mix the spring onion, butter and white wine vinegar
5. Pour the butter mix over the sprouts just before serving
   Serve as a side for meat or fish.

ROASTED TOMATOES WITH BASIL

(SERVES 2)
NUTRITION PER SERVING: CALORIES 30 | FAT 1G | CARBS 3G | PROTEIN 2G

INGREDIENTS:

◆ 4 medium tomatoes
◆ 8 cherry tomatoes
◆ 4g dried basil
◆ Salt and pepper to season
◆ 5–10ml oil

PREPARATION:

1. Preheat your air fryer to 180 degrees
2. Slice the larger tomatoes in half
3. Leave the cherry tomatoes whole
4. Sprinkle half the basil and seasoning over the tomatoes and spray with oil then turn them and sprinkle the rest of the seasoning and oil
5. Arrange in the air fryer basket and cook for 10 minutes turning halfway through
   Serve as a side with steak or salmon.

CORN ON THE COB

(SERVES 4)

NUTRITION PER SERVING: CALORIES 15 | FAT 0.5G | CARBS 1G | PROTEIN 0.5G

INGREDIENTS:

- 2 corn cobs
- 5–10ml oil

PREPARATION:

1. Preheat your fryer to 180 degrees
2. Remove the husk from the cob and cut each cob into 2 pieces widthways
3. Arrange the cobs in the air fryer basket and spray with the oil
4. Cook for 12–15 minutes shaking the basket every 3–4 minutes until they are beginning to brown
5. Lift out of the basket and serve hot

   For added indulgence place a knob of butter on each cob.

POTATO CRISPS

(SERVES 6)

NUTRITION PER SERVING: CALORIES 150 | FAT 1G | CARBS 8G | PROTEIN 1G

INGREDIENTS:

- ◆ 2 large potatoes
- ◆ 8g dried mixed herbs
- ◆ 2g sea salt
- ◆ 5ml oil

PREPARATION:

1. Peel and slice the potatoes thinly (A mandolin is great for slicing the potatoes for this recipe)
2. Soak the potato slices in water for 30 minutes
3. Drain and pat dry
4. Preheat your air fryer to 180 degrees
5. Spray the potato slices with oil on both sides
6. Mix the salt and dried herbs and sprinkle the mixture onto both sides of the slices
7. Arrange the slices in the air fryer basket and cook in batches for 15 minutes each until crisp, shaking the basket every 3–4 minutes. Be careful not to overcook

SAVOURY MUFFINS

(SERVES 4)

NUTRITION PER SERVING: CALORIES 200 | FAT 7G | CARBS 1G | PROTEIN 2G

INGREDIENTS:

- 45ml melted butter
- 2 grated garlic cloves
- 2 eggs
- 100g soured cream
- 120g almond flour
- 50g plain flour (Use another type of flour such as coconut flour if you prefer)
- 2g baking powder
- 120g grated Cheddar cheese
- 4g dried parsley
- 2g dried basil
- 2g dried rosemary
- 5–10ml oil

PREPARATION:

1. Preheat your air fryer to 160 degrees
2. Spray oil evenly over individual muffin cups
3. Beat the eggs and mix with the cream, garlic and salt
4. Mix the dry ingredients and the cheese together with your hands until a dough forms
5. Mix the dough with the egg mixture until everything is evenly blended (Blitz in a mixer if it's easier)
6. Pour the batter into the tray or individual muffin cups and top a little melted butter
7. Cook for 25 minutes until the tops are golden brown
8. Remove from the fryer and cool before serving

   Cut in half and spread with butter to serve. Serve as a side with soup.

SPICY POTATOES

(SERVES 4)

NUTRITION PER SERVING: CALORIES 97 | FAT 4G | CARBS 15G | PROTEIN 1G

INGREDIENTS:

- 4 large red potatoes (Desirée potatoes are good for this recipe)
- 4g garlic powder
- 14g smoked paprika
- 2g cayenne pepper
- 10ml oil
- Salt and pepper to season

PREPARATION:

1. Peel and roughly chop the potatoes into bite-size chunks
2. Parboil for 5 minutes in salted water and then rinse with cold water
3. Leave the potatoes to cool and soak up any moisture with kitchen roll
4. Preheat your air fryer to 200 degrees
5. Mix the ingredients in a bowl
6. Toss the potato chunks in the spicy mixture making sure they are evenly coated
7. Spray the potato chunks with oil
8. Arrange in the air fryer basket and cook for 15 minutes shaking the basket every 5 minutes. Check that the potatoes are done with a knife and cook for 5 more minutes if necessary
   Serve as a side for any meat or fish dish.

CRISPY ROAST POTATOES

(SERVES 4)

NUTRITION PER SERVING: CALORIES 220 | FAT 3G |CARBS 26G | PROTEIN 3G

INGREDIENTS:

- ◆ 4 large peeled and chopped Maris Piper potatoes
- ◆ 10ml oil

PREPARATION:

1. Preheat your air fryer to 180 degrees
2. Parboil the potatoes for 5 minutes
3. Drain well and rinse in cold water
4. Pat the potato pieces dry and spray with the oil
5. Arrange the potato piece in the air fryer basket and cook for 30 minutes shaking the basket every 5 minutes
   Serve with any meat or fish dish.

AVOCADO FRIES

(SERVES 4)

NUTRITION PER SERVING: CALORIES 160 | FAT 9G | CARBS 20G | PROTEIN 4.5G

INGREDIENTS:

◆ 2 large, sliced avocados (Slice the avocados lengthwise – you should get around 8 slices per avocado)

◆ 110g flour

◆ 230g breadcrumbs

◆ 10ml water

◆ 5ml lemon juice

◆ 2 eggs

◆ 10ml oil

◆ Salt and pepper to season

PREPARATION:

1. Preheat the air fryer to 200 degrees
2. Mix the dry ingredients in a bowl
3. Beat the egg and mix the water and lemon juice in a second bowl
4. Dip the avocado slices into the flour mixture and then the egg mixture making sure that they are fully coated
5. Carefully lay the slices onto the breadcrumbs, coating both sides
6. Spray the slices with oil making sure they are evenly covered
7. Arrange the avocado slices in the air fryer basket leaving gaps for the hot air to circulate
8. Cook for 8 minutes shaking the basket halfway through
   Serve as a snack with a dipping sauce or as a side.

SPICY CHICKEN WINGS

(SERVES 4)

NUTRITION PER SERVING: CALORIES 206 | FAT 15G | CARBS 1G | PROTEIN 18G

INGREDIENTS:

- 1kg chicken wings
- 14g of garam masala seasoning
- 5–10ml oil

PREPARATION:

1. Preheat your air fryer to 180 degrees
2. Trim off the tips of the chicken wings using scissors
3. Coat the wings in the oil and seasoning
4. Arrange in the air fryer and cook for 20–25 minutes shaking the basket every 5 minutes
5. When they are cooked the meat should easily come away from the bone
6. Remove from the fryer and serve immediately while still crisp
   Serve with any dip of your choice – maybe sour cream or a cucumber raita.

SPROUT AND BACON HASH

(SERVES 4)

NUTRITION PER SERVING: CALORIES 210 | FAT 3G | CARBS 1G | PROTEIN 4G

INGREDIENTS:

- 6 rashers chopped cooked bacon
- 1 chopped and diced onion
- 160g quartered Brussels sprouts
- 2 large green peppers
- 2 grated garlic cloves
- 4 eggs
- Salt and pepper to season
- 5ml oil

PREPARATION:

1. Preheat your air fryer to 180 degrees
2. Spray an air fryer baking tin with the oil
3. Mix all the ingredients together in a bowl
4. Pour into the baking tin and cook for 25 minutes
5. Cut the hash into portions and serve while hot

BACON ROLLS

(SERVES 6)

NUTRITION PER ROLL: CALORIES 260 | FAT 30G | CARBS 40G | PROTEIN 20G

INGREDIENTS:

- ◆ 12 bacon rashers
- ◆ 6 white rolls

PREPARATION:

1. Preheat your air fryer to 200 degrees
2. Arrange the rashers in the air fryer basket or on a tray (You won't need oil as there is already fat in the bacon)
3. Cook for 10–15 minutes depending on the level of crispiness you like. Shake or rearrange every 5 minutes until cooked
4. Lift out of your air fryer and place on kitchen towel to soak up any excess fat
5. Put the bacon into the bread rolls while still hot
   Add any ketchup of your choice.

AMERICAN STYLE GRILLED-CHEESE SANDWICH

(SERVES 1)

NUTRITION PER SERVING: CALORIES 429 | FAT 28G | CARBS 25G | PROTEIN 18G

INGREDIENTS:

- 3 slices Cheddar cheese
- 10ml mayonnaise
- 2 slices sandwich bread
- 5ml oil

PREPARATION:

1. Preheat your air fryer to 180 degrees
2. Arrange the cheese and mayonnaise inside the slices of bread to make the sandwich
3. Spray both sides of the sandwich with oil
4. Arrange on the air fryer tray or in the basket if it's big enough to lie flat and cook for 8 minutes turning halfway through

Meat and Fish Dishes

CHICKEN FAJITAS

(SERVES 4)

NUTRITION PER SERVING: CALORIES 235 | FAT 2G | CARBS 2G | PROTEIN 10G

INGREDIENTS:

- 2 sliced peppers (Any colour although the yellow and orange ones tend to be sweeter)
- 1 sliced onion
- 450g of chicken breast meat
- 20g of fajita seasoning. Add more, or less, depending on how spicy you like your food (You'll find jars of powdered fajita seasoning in supermarkets and most farm shops)
- 5–10ml of oil

PREPARATION:

1. Preheat your air fryer to 180 degrees
2. Slice the chicken into strips of about half a 2cm in width
3. In a bowl, coat the sliced chicken and vegetables with the fajita seasoning and spay with the oil
4. Arrange the mixture into an air fryer bowl or basket
5. Cook for 15–18 minutes. Shake the basket half way through. Check after 15 minutes and if necessary cook for another 5 minutes to crisp up

   Serve in tortilla wraps with sour cream or guacamole. Alternatively, serve on a bed of rice.

BARBECUE CHICKEN THIGHS

(SERVES 3)

NUTRITION PER SERVING: CALORIES 250 | FAT 21G | CARBS 5G | PROTEIN 30G

INGREDIENTS:
- 6 chicken thighs with skin on
- 5ml oil
- 14g of plain flour
- 14g of barbecue seasoning

PREPARATION:
1. Preheat your air fryer to 180 degrees
2. Spray the chicken thighs with the oil
3. Mix together the flour and seasoning and rub into the chicken thighs
4. Arrange the thighs in your air fryer and cook for 30 minutes turning halfway through
5. When the chicken is cooked the meat should come away from the bone easily. If there is any pink meat cook for another 5–10 minutes

   Serve with air fryer potato fries or salad.

CHICKEN GOUJONS

(SERVES 4)

NUTRITION PER SERVING: 170 CALORIES | FAT 9G | CARBS 0G | PROTEIN 8G

INGREDIENTS:

- 500g chicken breast meat
- 60g mayonnaise
- 20g mustard
- 30ml full fat milk
- 40g bacon powder
- 5ml oil

PREPARATION:

1. Preheat your air fryer to 200 degrees
2. Line the air fryer tray with foil or parchment and spay with the oil
3. Cut the chicken into 5/6 cm strips – no thicker than 2 cm
4. Mix the mayonnaise, mustard and milk in a bowl
5. Rub the mayonnaise mixture into the goujons and then coat them with the bacon powder
6. Arrange the goujons on the air fryer tray and cook for 15 minutes turning halfway through

   Serve with air fryer potato fries or salad.

ITALIAN MEATBALLS

(SERVES 4)

NUTRITION PER SERVING: CALORIES 150 | FAT 8G | CARBS 2G | PROTEIN 8G

INGREDIENTS:

- 500g minced beef
- 25g grated Parmesan
- 80g breadcrumbs
- 10g onion powder
- 2g Italian seasoning
- 10g dried parsley
- 1 egg
- 30ml milk
- 5–10ml oil
- Salt and pepper to season

PREPARATION:

1. Preheat your air fryer to 190 degrees
2. Mix the dry ingredients in a bowl
3. Add the mince, the beaten egg, and milk and mix well. (This is best done with your hands)
4. Divide the mixture into 16 meatballs of equal size and spray with the oil
5. Place the meatballs in the fryer basket in a single layer (You may have to cook these in batches)
6. Cook for 12–14 minutes shaking the basket halfway through
7. Lift the meatballs out and leave to rest before serving

   Serve with a thick, Italian tomato sauce and spaghetti. (Ready-made sauces are available in most supermarkets.)Top with more grated Parmesan.

STUFFED PEPPERS

(SERVES 2)

NUTRITION PER SERVING: CALORIES 250 | FAT 10G | CARBS 9G | PROTEIN 25G

INGREDIENTS:

- 4 green peppers
- 450g lean minced beef
- 50g finely chopped spring onion
- 60g grated mozzarella
- 250g cooked rice
- 250ml readymade tomato and basil sauce (Most supermarkets have fresh sauces in the chilled aisle. One of these is perfect for this recipe)
- 2 grated garlic cloves
- 2g dried sage
- 2g dried basil
- 15ml olive oil
- 5ml oil
- Salt and pepper to season

PREPARATION:

1. Fry the mince in a little oil until browned
2. Drain the meat and return to the pan
3. Stir in the spring onion, sage, basil, oil and seasoning and mix well
4. Add the tomato and basil sauce and cooked rice
5. Stir until the ingredients are evenly blended
6. Cut the tops off the peppers and scoop out the seeds
7. Stuff each pepper with an equal amount of the mixture
8. Spray some oil around the inside of the air fryer basket and line with parchment, making holes so that the hot air can circulate
9. Arrange the peppers in the basket and cook for 10 minutes
10. Open the fryer and add the grated mozzarella and cook for 5 more minutes

    Serve with a glass of chilled white wine.

AIR FRYER STEAK

(SERVES 2)

NUTRITION PER SERVING: CALORIES 220 | FAT 15G | CARBS 2G | PROTEIN 25G

INGREDIENTS:

- 2 sirloin steaks (Or any steaks of your choice)
- 5–10ml oil
- Plenty of salt and pepper to season

PREPARATION:

1. Season the steaks with salt and pepper and leave to rest for 30 minutes
2. Preheat your air fryer to 200 degrees
3. Line an air fryer tray with parchment
4. Spray the steaks with the oil on both sides
5. Arrange on the tray and cook for 5–6 minutes turning half way through
6. Remove from the fryer and rest before serving
   Serve with a sauce of your choice and air fryer potato fries.

GARLIC PORK CHOPS

(SERVES 4)

NUTRITION PER SERVING: CALORIES 210 | FAT 9G | CARBS 2G | PROTEIN 20G

INGREDIENTS:

- 4 pork chops
- 1 thinly sliced courgette
- 250g asparagus
- 30g garlic powder
- 10g dried oregano
- 30ml oil
- Juice of one lemon
- Salt and pepper to season

PREPARATION:

1. Mix the oil, lemon juice, garlic powder and oregano in a bowl
2. Coat the chops with the mixture and leave in the bowl
3. Cover the bowl and put in the fridge to marinade for 1 hour
4. Preheat your air fryer to 200 degrees
5. Spray the air fryer tray with the oil and line with parchment
6. Place the chops on the tray and pour over any remaining marinade
7. Arrange the sliced courgette and asparagus around the chops
8. Cook for 20 minutes turning the chops and rearranging the vegetables halfway through
9. If some of the meat is still pink, remove the vegetables and cook for a further 5 minutes
10. Lift the chops from the fryer and allow to rest before serving
    Serve with roasted or new potatoes. Add a creamy sauce for added indulgence.

ROAST PORK LOIN

(SERVES 6)

NUTRITION PER SERVING: CALORIES 220 | FAT 6G | CARBS 0G | PROTEIN 10G

INGREDIENTS:

- 1kg pork loin joint with the rind on
- 4g sea salt
- 2 grated garlic cloves
- 4g dried mixed herbs
- 5ml oil

PREPARATION:

1. Preheat your air fryer to 180 degrees
2. Score the rind with a sharp knife making 3–4 deep cuts
3. Mix the salt, garlic and mixed herbs and rub the mixture into the pork rind making sure to fill the scored sections
4. Spray the pork with the oil
5. Place the joint in the air fryer basket and cook for 50 minutes (or 25 minutes per 450g) shaking the basket every 10 minutes. Check the meat is cooked with a meat thermometer – it should be at least 65 degrees
6. Remover the pork from the fryer and rest for 10 minutes
   Serve with apple sauce and air fryer roast potatoes.

CHEESE AND HAM FRITTATA

(SERVES 2)

NUTRITION PER SERVING: CALORIES 284 | FAT 20G | CARBS 2G | PROTEIN 10G

INGREDIENTS:

- 4 eggs
- 20ml milk
- 100g grated cheese
- 2 thick slices of ham cut or torn into pieces
- 5ml oil
- Salt and pepper to season

PREPARATION:

1. Preheat your air fryer to 180 degrees
2. Spray the baking tin with the oil and line the bottom with parchment to avoid the frittata sticking
3. Beat the eggs and add the milk
4. Stir in the cheese and pieces of ham
5. Pour into the baking tin and cook for 15–20 minutes
6. Lift out of the tin and cut into 2 pieces
   Serve with air fryer potato fries or salad.

HERBY BREADED FISH

(SERVES 4)

NUTRITION PER SERVING: CALORIES 150G | FAT 3G | CARBS 6G | PROTEIN 10G

INGREDIENTS:

- 4 cod fillets
- 220g breadcrumbs
- 15g dried mixed herbs
- 50ml oil

PREPARATION:

1. Preheat your air fryer to 175 degrees
2. Mix the breadcrumbs, herbs and oil in a bowl
3. Beat the egg
4. Dip each cod fillet into the beaten egg and then the breadcrumb mixture
5. Spray the fillets with the oil and cook for 12 minutes turning the fish halfway through
6. Lift the fillets from the fryer and lay on kitchen towel to soak up any excess fat

   Serve with creamy tartare sauce and potato fries or with a wedge of lemon and roasted vegetables.

PAPRIKA SALMON FILLETS

(SERVES 2)

NUTRITION PER SERVING: CALORIES 180 | FAT 2G | CARBS 1G | PROTEIN 14G

INGREDIENTS:

- 2 salmon fillets
- 8g paprika seasoning
- 10ml oil

PREPARATION:

1. Preheat your air fryer to 190 degrees
2. Mix the oil and the paprika in a small bowl and rub onto the top of the salmon fillets
3. Arrange the fillets in the air fryer basket and cook for 5 minutes. Continue cooking and checking at 2 minute intervals until the salmon is ready

   Serve with roasted vegetables and/or new potatoes.

GARLIC AND LEMON PLAICE

(SERVES 2)

NUTRITION PER SERVING: CALORIES 160 | FAT 1G | CARBS 4G | PROTEIN 15G

INGREDIENTS:

- 2 large plaice fillets (You can use any white fish for this recipe but if you use more chunky fish such as haddock or cod allow a little extra cooking time)
- 2 grated garlic cloves
- 10ml lemon juice
- 2g onion powder
- 4g dried parsley
- 5ml oil
- Salt and pepper to season

PREPARATION:

1. Preheat your fryer to 180 degrees
2. Pat the fish dry
3. Mix the dry ingredients in a bowl and rub the mixture into both sides of the fillets with your hands
4. Spray the fillets with the lemon juice
5. If you have room to cook the fillets in the air fryer basket, spray the inside of the basket with the oil. If not, spray the air fryer tray with the oil and line with parchment
6. Arrange the fillets in the basket/on the tray and cook for 8–10 minutes turning halfway through
7. Lift out of the fryer and serve hot
   Serve with air fryer potato fries and a glass of chilled white wine.

TOMATO AND HERB TUNA STEAK

(SERVES 2)

NUTRITION PER SERVING: CALORIES 320 | FAT 8G | CARBS 1.5G | PROTEIN 20G

INGREDIENTS:

- 2 tuna steaks
- 15ml extra virgin olive oil
- 125g cherry tomatoes
- 4g dried basil
- 2g dried thyme
- 2g dried oregano
- 5ml oil
- Salt and pepper to season

PREPARATION:

1. Season the tuna steaks with the herbs and salt and pepper (Keep some of the basil back to season the tomatoes)
2. Leave to rest for 10 minutes in the fridge
3. Preheat your air fryer to 190 degrees
4. Pour the extra virgin olive oil over the tomatoes and sprinkle with the rest of the basil
5. Spray the inside of the air fryer basket with the oil
6. Lay the tuna steaks in the basket and arrange the tomatoes around them
7. Cook for 7–10 minutes turning the steaks halfway through (If they are large steaks allow another 5 minutes or so)
8. Check the steaks are cooked using a temperature probe. They should be at least 65 degrees

    Serve with new potatoes or air fryer roast potatoes.

TUNA FISH CAKES

(SERVES 4)

NUTRITION PER SERVING: CALORIES 250 | FAT 6G | CARBS 1G | PROTEIN 10G

INGREDIENTS:

- 140g tinned, drained tuna
- 60g bacon powder
- 5g dried herbs
- 110g grated cheese
- 7g mayonnaise
- 1 beaten egg
- 10ml water
- 10ml oil

PREPARATION:

1. Preheat your air fryer to 190 degrees
2. Mix all the ingredients except the oil together in a bowl (It's best to use your hands for this)
3. Make 8 equally sized fish cakes and spray with the oil
4. Arrange the fish cakes in the fryer basket (It's probably best to do these in 2 batches unless you have a large fryer)
5. Cook for 8 minutes shaking the bowl halfway through
   Serve with air fryer potato fries or salad.

LEMON PRAWNS

(SERVES 2)

NUTRITION PER SERVING: CALORIES 190 | FAT 4G | CARBS 6G | PROTEIN 15G

INGREDIENTS:

- 350g uncooked prawns
- 10ml lemon juice
- 1 lemon
- 2g garlic powder
- 15ml oil
- Salt and pepper to season

PREPARATION:

1. Preheat your air fryer to 200 degrees
2. Mix the ingredients in a bowl
3. Spay the air fryer bowl with the oil
4. Arrange the prawns in the basket and cook for 6–7 minutes shaking the basket every few minutes
5. Lift the prawns out with a spoon and soak up any excess fat with kitchen roll
6. Serve while hot
   Serve with mayonnaise in a jacket potato or with salad.

GARLIC SCALLOPS

(SERVES 2)

NUTRITION PER SERVING: CALORIES 250 | FAT 6G | CARBS 2G | PROTEIN 12G

INGREDIENTS:

- 8 cleaned and dried jumbo scallops
- 50ml olive oil
- 30g dried parsley
- 1 clove grated garlic
- 8g finely chopped capers
- 1 lemon
- Salt and pepper to season

PREPARATION:

1. Preheat your air fryer to 200 degrees
2. Spray the scallops with the oil
3. Arrange the scallops in the air fryer basket and cook for 4 minutes shaking the basket halfway through
4. Mix all the other ingredients in a bowl and toss the scallops making sure they are evenly coated
5. Arrange in the fryer and cook for another 2 minutes
   Serve with a dipping sauce of your choice or salad.

TOMATO AND HERB SCALLOPS

(SERVES 2)

NUTRITION PER SERVING: CALORIES 250 | FAT 15G | CARBS 3G | PROTEIN 5G

INGREDIENTS:
- 8 scallops
- 180ml double cream
- 15ml tomato purée
- 300g spinach
- 1 grated garlic clove
- 14g dried basil
- 2g salt
- 2g pepper
- 5–10ml oil
- Salt and pepper to season

PREPARATION:

1. Line the air fryer tray with parchment
2. Arrange the spinach in an even layer
3. Spray the oil on both sides of the scallops and arrange on top of the spinach
4. Season with salt and pepper
5. Mix together the remaining ingredients and spoon over the spinach and scallops
6. Cook for 10 minutes until the sauce is at boiling point
7. Check that the scallops are cooked using a probe thermometer. They should be at least 65 degrees in the centre
   Serve with air fryer roast potatoes.

Vegetarian and Vegan

TWO-CHEESE OMELETTE

(SERVES 2)

NUTRITION PER SERVING: CALORIES 178 | FAT 15G | CARBS 1G | PROTEIN 7G

INGREDIENTS:

- 4 eggs
- 55g grated Cheddar cheese
- 55g cubed feta
- 25ml milk
- 5ml oil
- Salt and pepper to season

PREPARATION:

1. Preheat your air fryer to 180 degrees
2. Spray a baking tin with the oil and line the bottom with parchment to avoid the omelette sticking
3. Beat the eggs and add the milk
4. Add the cheese and mix well
5. Pour the mixture into the baking tin and cook for 15 minutes
6. Fold the omelette in half and lift out of your fryer
7. Cut into 2 pieces and serve
   Serve with air fryer potato fries or salad.

CHEESY STUFFED MUSHROOMS

(SERVES 4)
NUTRITION PER SERVING: CALORIES 230 | FAT 8G | CARBS 3G | PROTEIN 5G

INGREDIENTS:

- 8 large flat mushrooms (Stems removed)
- 80g finely chopped spring onions
- 170g cream cheese
- 60g grated Cheddar cheese
- 2g paprika powder
- 5–10ml oil
- Salt and pepper to season

PREPARATION:

1. Preheat your oven fryer to 190 degrees
2. Spray the air fryer basket with the oil and arrange the mushrooms in the air fryer basket and cook for 5 minutes (It might be better to cook in two batches)
3. Remove the mushrooms from the basket and drain away any water that has collected in the tray
4. Mix the cheese, spring onions, paprika and seasoning in a bowl
5. Fill each mushroom pressing the filling down with the back of a spoon
6. Arrange the mushrooms in the air fryer basket and cook for 10 minutes until golden brown
7. Remove from the fryer and serve while hot
   Serve with roasted vegetables or salad.

VEGETARIAN STUFFED AUBERGINE

(SERVES 4)
NUTRITION PER SERVING: CALORIES 220 | FAT 9G | CARBS 20G | PROTEIN 5G

INGREDIENTS:
- 8 small aubergines
- 90ml oil
- 1 finely chopped large onion
- 3 grated garlic cloves
- 4g dried thyme
- 4g dried oregano
- 4g dried basil
- 1 tin of chopped tomatoes
- 50g breadcrumbs
- 25g grated Parmesan
- 25g grated Cheddar cheese
- 5–10ml oil
- Salt and pepper to season

PREPARATION:

1. Preheat your air fryer to 160 degrees
2. Mix all the ingredients together in a bowl
3. Make 2 large cuts lengthwise in each aubergine and stuff with the filling using the back of a spoon to press the filling in
4. Spray the aubergines with the oil (5ml per batch if you are cooking in 2 batches)
5. Arrange the aubergines in the air fryer basket and cook for 15 minutes
6. Check the aubergines every 5 minutes after this until they are cooked

   Serve with salad or new potatoes.

AUBERGINE LASAGNE

(SERVES 4)

NUTRITION PER SERVING: CALORIES 180 | FAT 9G | CARBS 7G |PROTEIN 5G

INGREDIENTS:

- 1 large sliced aubergine
- 2 eggs
- 8 mozzarella cheese slices
- 220g readymade tomato and basil sauce (You will find this in the chilled aisle of the supermarket)
- 2g onion powder
- 2 grated cloves of garlic
- 2g dried basil
- 100g grated Parmesan
- 110g breadcrumbs
- 5–10ml oil

PREPARATION:

1. Preheat your air fryer to 185 degrees
2. Mix all the dry ingredients except the breadcrumbs together in a bowl
3. Beat the eggs in a separate bowl
4. Place the breadcrumbs in a third bowl
5. Toss the aubergine slices in the seasoning mix in the first bowl then dip each slice into the beaten egg
6. Finally, coat each slice with breadcrumbs and spray with oil
7. Arrange the slices in the air fryer basket and cook for 20 minutes turning halfway through
8. In a separate dish, arrange a layer of 4 aubergine slices followed by 4 mozzarella slices and then pour over half of the tomato sauce. Repeat a second time
9. Top with some more grated Parmesan and pop under the grill for a few minutes to brown
   Serve with garlic bread and salad.

MAC AND CHEESE

(SERVES 4)

NUTRITION PER SERVING: CALORIES 210 | FAT 8G | CARBS 16G | PROTEIN 10G

INGREDIENTS:

- 250g macaroni pasta
- 250g grated cheese
- 650ml milk
- 2 grated garlic cloves
- 10g dried oregano
- Salt and pepper to season

PREPARATION:

1. Preheat your air fryer to 160 degrees
2. Mix the ingredients together in a bowl
3. Spray a baking tin with the oil and pour in the mixture
4. Cook for 18 minutes stirring every 3–4 minutes or continue until cooked
5. Spoon into four bowls to serve and sprinkle with a little more grated cheese or Parmesan

    Great eaten straight from the bowl with and accompanied by a glass of chilled white wine.

CHEESE AND ONION LOADED POTATO SKINS

(SERVES 2)

NUTRITION PER SERVING: CALORIES 220 | FAT 9G | CARBS 26G | PROTEIN 5G

INGREDIENTS:

- 8 small potatoes (Around 4 cm in width is best for this recipe)
- 30ml low-fat sour cream
- 28g grated Cheddar cheese
- 4 finely chopped and sliced spring onions
- 10ml oil

PREPARATION:

1. Preheat your air fryer to 180 degrees
2. Spray the potatoes with oil and arrange them in the air fryer basket and cook for 25 minutes until soft all the way through
3. Mix the other ingredients together
4. Lift the potatoes out of the fryer and place on a serving plate
5. Cut them open and place an equal amount of filling in each potato

   Delicious with a glass of chilled white wine.

SPICY HALOUMI BALLS

(SERVES 4)

NUTRITION PER SERVING: CALORIES 210 | FAT 4G | CARBS 5G | PROTEIN 8G

INGREDIENTS:

- 110g cubed haloumi
- 4g smoked paprika
- 2g brown sugar
- 2g mustard
- 2g cornflour
- 2 grated garlic cloves
- 1 egg
- 30g breadcrumbs
- 2g dried herbs
- 5–10ml oil

PREPARATION:

1. Mix the dry ingredients in a bowl and toss the haloumi cubes until they are evenly coated
2. Beat the egg and coat the haloumi
3. Arrange on a tray and chill for 30 minutes in the fridge
4. Preheat your air fryer to 180 degrees
5. Arrange the haloumi in the air fryer basket, spray with the oil and cook for 6–8 minutes until golden shaking the basket halfway through
6. Serve while hot

   Serve with a hot and spicy dipping sauce.

VEGAN SWEET AND SOUR TOFU

(SERVES 4)

NUTRITION PER SERVING: CALORIES 190 | FAT 5G | CARBS 12G | PROTEIN 5G

INGREDIENTS:

- 400g cubed tofu drained and dried (It's always best to use extra firm tofu in the air fryer for a better texture when cooked)
- 50ml fresh orange juice
- 16ml honey
- 5ml rice vinegar
- 2g corn powder
- 30ml soy sauce
- 115g brown rice
- 14 toasted sesame seeds
- 4 chopped spring onions
- 15ml oil
- Salt and pepper to season

PREPARATION:

1. Preheat your air fryer to 170 degrees
2. Spray the tofu with the oil
3. Arrange the tofu pieces in the air fryer basket and cook for 10 minutes shaking the basket halfway through
4. Meanwhile mix together the other ingredients in a saucepan and heat until the sauce thickens
5. Stir the tofu into the sauce and serve with the brown rice

VEGAN BEAN PATTIES

(SERVES 4)

NUTRITION PER SERVING: CALORIES 170 | FAT 1G | CARBS 25G | PROTEIN 8G

INGREDIENTS:

- 1 400g tin beans (Use black beans or any beans of your choice)
- 280g rolled oats (Blitz in a blender to grind more finely or buy them ready ground)
- 1 small tin sweetcorn
- 2g garlic powder
- 1g chilli powder
- 15ml soy sauce
- 180ml salsa sauce
- 5ml oil

PREPARATION:

1. Drain the beans and the sweetcorn
2. Mix all the ingredients together in a bowl with your hands until the mixture is evenly blended
3. Cover the bowl and put the bean mixture in the fridge for at least 15 minutes
4. Preheat your air fryer to 180 degrees
5. Shape the bean mixture into 4 patties
6. Spray the oil inside the air fryer basket and line with parchment. Make sure there are holes in the parchment for the air to circulate
7. Arrange the patties in the basket and cook for 15 minutes turning halfway through. Keep an eye on them after 10 minutes as you don't want them to dry out
   Serve in a bun or with salad.

VEGAN AVOCADO WRAPS

(SERVES 4)
NUTRITION PER SERVING: CALORIES 110 | FAT 5G | CARBS 2G | PROTEIN 5G

INGREDIENTS:

- 8 vegan egg-roll wrappers
- 3 mashed avocados
- ½ tin of chopped tomatoes
- 5ml oil
- Salt and pepper to season

PREPARATION:

1. Preheat your air fryer to 180 degrees
2. Mix the ingredients together in a bowl
3. Lay out the egg-roll wrappers and fill each one, folding corner to corner and then wrapping, sealing the sides with water
4. Spray the wraps with 10ml oil
5. Arrange in the air fryer basket and cook for 5 minutes until crispy shaking the bowl halfway through
   Serve with a dipping sauce of your choice.

VEGAN MEXICAN WRAPS

(SERVES 2)

NUTRITION PER SERVING: CALORIES 150 | FAT 4G | CARBS 6G | PROTEIN 6G

INGREDIENTS:

- 2 vegan Mexican tortillas
- 60g pinto beans (Or use any beans of your choice)
- 60g grated vegan cheese
- 5/6 iceberg lettuce leaves
- 2 sliced avocados
- 60ml readymade salsa
- 5–10ml oil

PREPARATION:

1. Preheat your air fryer to 180 degrees
2. Arrange the following ingredients on each tortilla: beans, grated cheese, salsa, lettuce leaves and avocado slices. Make sure to leave space around the edge for folding
3. Fold the tortillas bringing each corner into the middle. Allow some overlap and press some grated cheese into the join to seal as the tortillas cook
4. Spray the tortillas with the oil
5. Arrange in the air fryer basket and cook for 6 minutes turning halfway through until crispy
   Serve with sour cream.

CRISPY VEGAN RAVIOLI

(SERVES 4)

NUTRITION PER SERVING: CALORIES 180 | FAT 0.5G | CARBS 5G | PROTEIN 2G

INGREDIENTS:

- 115g breadcrumbs
- 8g yeast flakes
- 4g dried basil
- 4g dried oregano
- 2 grated garlic cloves
- 60ml aquafaba liquid (Liquid drained from a tin of chickpeas or other beans will do just as well)
- 225g vegan ravioli filled with any filling of your choice (Find this in the chilled aisle of the supermarket)
- 150ml readymade Italian tomato sauce (Also find this in the chilled aisle of the supermarket)
- 10ml oil

PREPARATION:

1. Preheat your air fryer to 190 degrees
2. Mix the dry ingredients in a bowl
3. Put the aquafaba in a separate bowl
4. Put the ravioli in the aquafaba and lift out with a slotted spoon
5. Coat the ravioli in the dry ingredients by mixing them in the bowl using your hands
6. Spray the ravioli with the oil
7. Arrange in the air fryer basket and cook for 8 minutes turning the ravioli halfway through
8. Lift the ravioli out of the basket and drain on kitchen roll
9. Warm the tomato sauce
10. Arrange on a plate and serve with a bowl of tomato sauce for dipping

VEGAN TOFU IN SESAME SAUCE

(SERVES 4)

NUTRITION PER SERVING: CALORIES 160 | FAT 2G | CARBS 12G | PROTEIN 6G

INGREDIENTS:

- 400g extra firm drained and dried tofu
- 60ml orange juice
- 28g finely chopped spring onions
- 14 toasted sesame seeds
- 15ml honey
- 5ml rice vinegar
- 2g cornflour
- 50ml soy sauce
- 115g brown rice
- Salt and pepper to season
- 5ml oil

PREPARATION:

1. Preheat your air fryer to 180 degrees
2. Dice the tofu and spray with the oil making sure there is an even coating
3. Arrange the tofu in the air fryer basket and cook for 15 minutes shaking the basket every 5 minutes
4. Remove the tofu and keep warm until the rice and sauce are ready
5. Cook the rice for 10–15 minutes in a saucepan of boiling water
6. Put all the other ingredients except the rice into a saucepan and stir until thickened
7. Combine the tofu with the sauce and serve with brown rice

Sweet Snacks and Desserts

BANANA BREAD

(SERVES 6)

NUTRITION PER SERVING: CALORIES 300 | FAT 8G | CARBS 15G | PROTEIN 4G

INGREDIENTS:

- 85g flour
- 3g baking powder
- 110g granulated sugar
- 4g cinnamon
- 2 eggs
- 2 mashed, ripe bananas
- 120g plain yoghurt
- 5ml vanilla essence
- 110g chopped walnuts

PREPARATION:

1. Preheat your air fryer to 150 degrees
2. Spray the baking tin with the oil and line with parchment
3. Mix the dry ingredients in a bowl
4. Beat the egg and mix with the yoghurt, mashed bananas, sugar, oil and vanilla in another bowl
5. Add the dry ingredients to the banana mixture and add the chopped walnuts
6. Stir gently
7. Pour the banana bread mixture into the baking tin
8. Cook for 30 minutes or until brown (Check the bread is cooked by using a skewer. If it comes out clean, the banana bread is ready)
9. Lift the baking tin out of the fryer and turn the banana bread out onto a rack to cool

    Slice and serve with butter or place in a bowl and serve with custard.

LEMON SPONGE CAKE

(SERVES 6)

NUTRITION PER SERVING: CALORIES 310 | FAT 8G | CARBS 12G | PROTEIN 4G

INGREDIENTS:
- 100g plain flour
- 100g butter
- 100g caster sugar
- 2 eggs
- Juice and grated peel of 1 lemon
- Pinch of salt
- 4g of baking powder

PREPARATION:

1. Heat your air fryer to 180 degrees
2. Spray the baking tin with the oil and place some parchment in the bottom to avoid the cake sticking
3. Beat together the butter and sugar
4. Add the beaten eggs and mix
5. Add the flour, salt and lemon ingredients and stir until the mixture is smooth and creamy
6. Pour the mixture into the cake tin or bowl
7. Cook for 15 minutes then check whether the cake is cooked using a skewer. Push it into the centre of the cake – if it comes out clean then the cake is done. If not, cook for a further 5 minutes
8. Turn the cake out onto a rack to cool

   For added indulgence coat the top of the cake with lemon icing made from icing sugar mixed with a little water and lemon juice.

LUXURY CHOCOLATE LAVA CAKE

(SERVES 2)

NUTRITION PER SERVING: CALORIES 450 | FAT 29G | CARBS 43G | PROTEIN 6G

INGREDIENTS:

- 60g chocolate chips
- 55g butter
- 110g granulated sugar
- 1 egg + 1 egg yolk
- 36g plain flour
- 3ml vanilla essence
- Pinch salt

PREPARATION:

1. Preheat your air fryer to 175 degrees
2. Heat the chocolate chips and butter until melted and mix together
3. Beat the egg and the egg yolk and mix with the vanilla essence and salt
4. Add to the chocolate mixture and stir until smooth and fully blended
5. Add the flour and stir until the mixture is smooth
6. Spray the air fryer baking tin with the oil (Individual ramekins are better if you have them)
7. Cover the mix or individual ramekins with foil and cook for 8–10 minutes
8. Remove the foil and cook for another 5 minutes until the tops are crispy
9. Remove from the air fryer and leave to cool
   Serve with whipped cream or ice cream.

CINNAMON DONUTS

(MAKES AROUND 8 DONUTS)
NUTRITION PER DONUT: CALORIES 300G | FAT 15G | CARBS 18G | PROTEIN 1G

INGREDIENTS:

- 250g bread flour (You can use plain flour but bread flour makes a lighter donut as the dough will rise more)
- 15g sugar
- 15g cinnamon
- 7g dried yeast (1 sachet)
- A pinch salt
- 15ml melted butter
- 1 large egg
- 90ml warm milk

PREPARATION:

1. Mix the dry ingredients together in a bowl
2. Add the egg, milk and butter to a well in the centre of the flour mixture and stir gently until the dough has bound together into a ball
3. Turn the dough out onto a floured surface and knead for about 10–15 minutes until the dough has an elastic texture
4. Spray a bowl with oil and move the dough around in it until coated and then cover the bowl with cling film and leave somewhere warm to prove for about 45 minutes. When it is ready the dough should have doubled in size
5. Roll the dough out on a floured surface to around a 1 centimetre thickness
6. Using a cutter or drinking glass cut out around 8 circles of dough
7. Using a smaller cutter or maybe a shot glass cut out the centres of your donuts. They should now be ring shaped. Don't make the centre hole too small or they won't cook through
8. If you have time, cover the donuts and leave to rise for a second time for about 30 minutes for extra fluffiness
9. Heat your air fryer to 225 degrees
10. Baste each donut with melted butter and place in the fryer basket. Cook for 5 minutes and then turn and cook for a further 2 minutes (You will probably need to cook the donuts in batches)
11. Remove the donuts from the fryer and allow to cool

For added indulgence, brush each donut with melted butter and dip into a sugar and cinnamon mixture.

CHOCOLATE CHIP BISCUITS

(SERVES 12)

NUTRITION PER SERVING: CALORIES 320 | FAT 14G | CARBS 18G | PROTEIN 4G

INGREDIENTS:

- 115g melted butter
- 40g granulated sugar
- 10ml vanilla essence
- 1 beaten egg
- 190g plain flour
- 2g salt
- 2g baking powder
- 120g chocolate chips

PREPARATION:

1. Preheat your air fryer to 170 degrees
2. Line the air fryer tray with parchment
3. Beat the butter and sugar together in a bowl
4. Add the egg and vanilla essence and mix to form a batter
5. Stir in the flour, baking powder and salt until the texture of the batter is creamy
6. Add the chocolate chips and fold until they are evenly distributed through the mixture
7. Arrange 12 scoops of evenly spaced biscuit dough on the tray, leaving 5 cm between each one (Cook in 2 batches of 6 if necessary)
8. Cook for 8–10 minutes until golden brown
9. Leave the biscuits to harden on the tray before moving
   Store in an airtight container.

KEY LIME CHEESECAKE

(SERVES 12)

NUTRITION PER SERVING: CALORIES 380 | FAT 15G | CARBS 22G | PROTEIN 3G

INGREDIENTS:

- 750g soft cream cheese
- 75g melted butter
- 400g caster sugar
- 3 eggs
- 50ml Greek yoghurt
- 15ml vanilla essence
- 90g crushed biscuits (Ginger biscuits work well with this recipe)
- Zest and juice of 8 limes

PREPARATION:

1. Preheat your air fryer to 160 degrees
2. Spray the baking tin with the oil and line with parchment (If you have a springform pan the cheesecake will be easier to remove at the end)
3. Mix the crushed biscuits with the butter using your hands
4. Place the biscuit mixture in the pan and press down firmly to make the cheesecake base
5. Beat the sugar and cream cheese until smooth
6. Add the yoghurt, vanilla essence and lime ingredients, and beat again until smooth
7. Beat the eggs and stir in until fully absorbed into the mixture
8. Pour the batter into the baking tin on top of the biscuit base
9. Cook for 30 minutes and leave to cool in the baking tin for a further 30 minutes
10. Chill the cheesecake in the fridge overnight before removing from the baking tin
11. Decorate with more lime zest
    Serve with clotted cream for extra indulgence.

CHOCOLATE BROWNIES

(SERVES 4)

NUTRITION PER SERVING: CALORIES 350 | FAT 17G | CARBS 33G | PROTEIN 7G

INGREDIENTS:
- 110g plain flour
- 84g unsweetened cocoa powder
- 170g sugar
- 60g unsalted butter
- 2 eggs
- 15ml oil
- 6ml vanilla essence
- 2g baking powder
- 5ml oil

PREPARATION:
1. Preheat your air fryer to 160 degrees
2. Spray the baking tin with the 5ml oil and line with parchment
3. Beat the eggs and mix all the ingredients together in a bowl until the batter is smooth
4. Pour the batter into the baking tin and cook for 15 minutes (Check that the brownies are done by inserting a knife or skewer. If it comes out clean, they're done)
5. Leave the brownie mixture to cool in the pan before slicing and serving
   Serve with cream or ice cream.

NUTTY GRANOLA

(SERVES 10)

NUTRITION PER SERVING: CALORIES 240 | FAT 15G | CARBS 28G | PROTEIN 6G

INGREDIENTS:
- 200g rolled oats
- 100g mixed chopped nuts (Use 2 or 3 different types of nuts for variety)
- 50g seeds (Again, use 2 or 3 types. Sunflower seeds work well in granola, as do pumpkin seeds)
- 50g dried fruit
- 120ml pouring honey
- 28g brown sugar
- 60ml melted butter
- 2 pinches of salt

PREPARATION:

1. Preheat your air fryer to 160 degrees
2. Line the basket with parchment making some holes for the air to circulate
3. Mix the seeds and nuts in a bowl
4. Add the honey and butter and mix thoroughly until all the nuts and seeds are coated
5. Pour the mixture into the basket and cook for 18 minutes shaking the basket every 5 minutes
6. When the mixture is cooked stir in the dried fruit
7. Spoon the granola on a tray to cool

   Serve with yoghurt or milk. Store the remainder of the granola in an airtight container.

NUTTY GRANOLA BARS

(SERVES 8)

NUTRITION PER SERVING: CALORIES 260 | FAT 8G | CARBS 0.5G | PROTEIN 15G

INGREDIENTS:

- 70g chopped almonds
- 35g chopped pecans
- 100g shredded coconut
- 25g dried fruit
- 25g chocolate chips
- 40g sunflower seeds
- 15g melted butter
- 15ml maple syrup
- 15g granulated sugar
- 4ml vanilla essence
- 1g salt

PREPARATION:

1. Preheat your air fryer to 150 degrees
2. Spray the air fryer tray with the oil and line with parchment
3. Blitz the coconut, nuts and sunflower seeds in a food processor until crumbly in texture
4. Mix with the fruit, chocolate chips and salt in a bowl
5. Mix the butter and maple syrup in a small saucepan over a low heat and stir in the sugar and vanilla essence
6. Pour the butter mix over the granola crumb and mix thoroughly using your hands
7. Pour the mixture onto the air fryer tray and press down until the mix is firm and even
8. Cook for 20 minutes until the edges start to brown (It's difficult to turn the granola but the parchment will stop it from sticking)
9. Remove the granola from the tray and place on a rack to cool
10. Cut into 8 slices and serve

CHOCOLATE SPONGE

(SERVES 6)

NUTRITION PER SERVING: CALORIES 300 | FAT 15G | CARBS 12G | PROTEIN 4G

INGREDIENTS:

- 175g plain flour
- 45g cocoa powder
- 5g baking powder
- 80g granulated sugar
- 60g butter
- 60ml milk
- 2 eggs
- 5ml vanilla essence
- 2g salt
- 5ml oil

PREPARATION:

1. Preheat your air fryer to 160 degrees
2. Spray the air fryer baking tin with the oil and line with parchment
3. Beat the butter and sugar in a bowl until smooth
4. Beat the eggs and add to the butter mixture with the milk and vanilla. Mix until you have a smooth batter
5. Mix the dry ingredients together in a separate bowl and fold in to the batter in stages until the cake mixture is smooth
6. Pour the cake batter into the baking tin and cook for 30 minutes
7. Cool for 30 minutes and then tip out of the tin and cut into sections Serve with custard or ice cream.

SPICED APPLE FRITTERS

(SERVES 4)

NUTRITION PER SERVING: CALORIES 250 | FAT 12G | CARBS 15G | PROTEIN 4G

INGREDIENTS:

- 4 peeled and sliced cooking apples
- 4g ground cinnamon
- 28g granulated sugar
- 2 eggs
- 2g baking powder
- 60ml milk
- 10ml lemon juice
- 5ml vanilla essence
- 225g plain flour
- Pinch salt
- 5ml oil

PREPARATION:

1. Preheat your air fryer to 175 degrees
2. Mix the dry ingredients in a bowl
3. Beat the eggs and stir in the milk, lemon juice and vanilla essence
4. Add the egg mixture to the dry ingredients and stir until smooth
5. Peel and chop the apples into wedges and dip each wedge into the batter
6. Arrange the fritters in the air fryer basket so that the hot air can circulate and spray with the oil
7. Cook for 10 minutes shaking the basket halfway through
8. Remove from the basket and lay on kitchen towel to soak up any oil
   Serve with pouring cream or ice cream.

LEMON SHORTBREAD

(SERVES 4)

NUTRITION PER SERVING: CALORIES 340 | FAT 15G | CARBS 12G | PROTEIN 4G

INGREDIENTS:

- 250g plain flour
- 30ml skimmed milk
- 110g unsalted butter
- 1 egg
- 110g granulated sugar
- 4g baking powder
- Zest and juice of 2 lemons
- Pinch of salt
- 5ml oil

PREPARATION:

1. Preheat your air fryer to 170 degrees
2. Cream together the butter and sugar
3. Beat the eggs and mix with the milk
4. Add the egg mixture to the butter and sugar and beat thoroughly until smooth
5. Stir in the flour, baking powder, salt, and lemon zest and peel
6. Mix until a dough has formed
7. Chill in the fridge for at least 30 minutes
8. Spray the air fryer tray with the oil and line with parchment
9. Roll out the dough on a floured surface until 1cm thick, then slice into 3cm strips to make the shortbread fingers
10. Arrange the shortbread fingers on the tray and cook for 15 minutes or until the shortbread has started to brown, checking after 10 minutes
11. Allow to cool on the tray before serving
    Serve as part of an afternoon tea.

Disclaimer

This book contains opinions and ideas of the author and is meant to teach the reader informative and helpful knowledge while due care should be taken by the user in the application of the information provided. The instructions and strategies are possibly not right for every reader and there is no guarantee that they work for everyone. Using this book and implementing the information/recipes therein contained is explicitly your own responsibility and risk. This work with all its contents, does not guarantee correctness, completion, quality or correctness of the provided information. Misinformation or misprints cannot be completely eliminated.

Printed in Great Britain
by Amazon